Also by L.R. Berger

Sightings
The Unexpected Aviary

Indebted to Wind

poems

L.R. Berger

DEERBROOK EDITIONS

PUBLISHED BY

Deerbrook Editions
P.O. Box 542
Cumberland. ME 04021
deerbrookeditions.com
Online catalogue: issuu.com/deerbrookeditions

FIRST EDITION

ISBN: 978-1-7368477-3-2
Book design by Jeffrey Haste
Cover photo, *Room to Breathe*, by Danielle D. Nelson

for Jessica

Contents

Indebted to Wind

Not what it had to say
but what it carried to you.

Dandelion silk dispatching seed.
The neighbor's trashcan lid

waking you from that nightmare
hurled in a tempest
against the bedroom window.

Howling, love cry,
lamentation.

Wind carries out the past and in
the future,

tutors your own breath
to extinguish the flame.

When love unbuttoned your blouse
wind did the rest
fumbling through the aspens.

You could have believed
air was empty space
to be lost in, except for wind

stinging your face
at the height of January,

whipping the flag,
lifting the sparrow.

I

First Acts

Filling the teapot at the tap,
turning on the burner—

praise be for the day's first acts
requiring no imagination,
no choices of consequence.

You can be half asleep
and already a success at life,

draw encouragement
mastering the rituals of morning—

parting the curtains, reuniting
with your eyeglasses.

The looming hurdles of the day
begin to loom possible,

the heavy head of the earth

will not today spin off
on its orbit without you.

The water boils and you know
what to do, your cold feet

anchored again
to the map of the world.

Picking Raspberries

This morning I went out to the garden with an empty white bowl
and walked back inside with an empty white bowl.

In between and without decorum, I ravaged the vines
of late July, plucked and shoveled
palmfuls of sweet fruit into my mouth.

Someone watching might have said,
now there's a woman whose body has slept alone
in a wide bed for a very long time.

My five-year-old godchild Ella
carried the empty white bowl for us yesterday
to pick raspberries for the first time.

It was left to me to explain about thorns.

We picked a few together, but then she disappeared
into her no-nonsense face, small fingers
threading thickets with intent.

From now on, she decreed after an uncommon
interlude of silence, *we are going to pick raspberries
every time I come.*

It was the end of the season.
It was left to me to explain about seasons.

What could I say to her unforgiving eyes?
With what conviction expound

on the virtues of going without sweetness
to a mouth full of sweetness?

Momentarily Untitled

What did I come into
this room for?

The name of that restaurant?
The street where she lives?

What was it no one told me?

The post office box
won't open with my house key.

I thought it was still August
but this is where I live.

What was it he said
that made me leave him?

Wasn't there a grudge?
Or two?

Who gifted me that carved
wooden monk on the windowsill?

Her first name started with a *G.*

Is my password still swallowtail?

That shrub, mock orange,
until I remember it's honeysuckle.

Weren't there always
mistaken identities?

Did we see that movie?
Did I enjoy it?

Were his dying words to me
everlasting joy

or *joy everlasting?*

Aurora's Actually

At four, she's found a word
to devote herself to.

I'm four and a half, actually.

A study in elocution, each syllable
bestowed with space and time.

Actually, that's not a beetle
it's a stinkbug. I don't like baths
and I hate spiders, actually.

Her small-fry body's
conferred with stature,

and with each *actually*
the face that goes with it.
Think Priestess. Delphic oracle.

What's a bouquet? she asks,
making one of purple clover.

They're not purple, she corrects me.
They're lavender, actually.

None of us knows
where she learned the word
or perfected its deployment.

We often don't know
how she knows what she knows.

Hers is a mind with a predilection
for precision. For truth,

actually.

So who can blame us
for standing chilled
in late August

swooning at the arcs
of barn swallows

when out of nowhere
she informs us

They will not be coming back
next year, actually.

Palliative Care
    for Hal

1.

What was going on in that room
was going on in that room.

Outside was the world
that is always on fire
and the world that always isn't.

But we were there, we were.
And God could sometimes be found

in your final watercolor
propped up and facing us
on the sill of the hospital window—

its suggestion of wintered trees
fracturing banks of blue

while under a tent of white sheet
you faded like fugitive colors.

2.

But not your eyes.

They were steady blue flares up ahead
on the gravel of night's back road.

Your smile, slightly askew,
still offering itself to everybody.

Wheeling toward you

through the revolving
glass hospital doors

all my formerly nursed concerns
were breathlessly confiscated.

3.

Sometimes the heft
of a word's true meaning
comes to find us.

Inside your room,
two windows, three chairs—
one word was *enough*.

But have I done enough good?
was the only *enough*
at first that concerned you

until weeks later
you rallied to protest
enough is enough.

Wearing the face of the jilted
you woke each morning
to find death stood you up.

Your doctor confiding, *Enough
to kill a horse*. Morphine enough.

4.

Tuesday you're a wooden broom.
Wednesday, a sleeping prince.

Fallen nestling, featherless,
still breathing splayed
on an asphalt driveway Thursday.

Saturday at dawn,
yours is the still living face
of Christ crucified.

Sometimes the heft
of a word's meaning
comes to find us.

Wind circling the hospital
with something like intention,

whirlpool of winter, Sunday,
refusing to lose its grip.

5.

For weeks I neglected the moon.
Walking home I never thought to look at the sky.

During the night I was dreaming
about birds we don't have. Nightingales.
Magpies. Cuckoos.

Whatever comes next
we'll have to cross

through an old-growth forest
to get there.

6.

One of our last conversations concerned color.

I pulled the cotton blouse from my closet
to offer your eyes a blurry swatch of blue.

Chicory-weed. Forget-me-nots.

What would we have done, you asked,
without the companionship of blue?

Then you looked off squinting, that fixing
of the eyes we hope sharpens our ears,
yours tuned now to other frequencies.

Someone's last breath down the corridor?
The tolling of stars? Vibrato of blue?

7.

The bouquet of dahlias I bought
weeks ago won't die.

*Do you really think it would be all right
if I let go of everything?*

Once you stopped breathing so long
I crossed the room
whispering *finale,* meaning *finally.*

Then you gasped like a newborn
gulping his first fist of air.

8.

Forty days and, no kidding, forty nights.

Sometimes the heft of a word's
true meaning comes to find us.

For awhile it was *affliction.*
But now it was *now.*

Whatever comes next
we'll have to cross

through an old-growth forest
to get there.

Virgin forest. Dappled light:
yours finally leaving us.

Blue Yonder

The geese are going places,
flying west in formation
low over the tidal marsh.

We're all going places,
some of us flying low
under evening's sky

closer to the place
we all end up going.

There was a time
I wanted to go with them—

watched them coursing south
across a late October field

in the dream I woke from
crying *Take me with you.*

My body that night, the place
they were passing through.

I can still hear them calling
though they've flown
out of sight like the dead

whom I also love, gone
to their unimaginable places.

Who knew I'd still be here,
at home, at last,
feet to good earth?

Good luck, I holler
with everything I've got—

no trace of longing
for any blue yonder.

Sheila's Marginalia

After she died, the books
that were her friends
went home with her friends.
I buckled mine
into the passenger seat
steering away from the home
where she'd always refused
any facts supporting
hopelessness, branding me
traitor for answering,
Yes, it's true what they say,
you are going to die now.

That's how it is
with the sturdy tugboat
women call friendship.
We haul in the oxygen tanks
and crack jokes
while redispensing
vomited medication.
We tell the kids,
we phone the ex-husband.
We declare bathing
incontestable and bawl
without apology. We tack
the note to her door
she dictates before leaving
on the stretcher for hospice:
Gone Fishing.

Surrounding the deathbed
we take all requests
for songs, for touch,
for chips of ice held to dry lips.

Sing that one again.
We hold the children,
we comfort the children.
We steal the rose
from the styrofoam cup
and strew its petals
down over the heart
waiting for the undertaker.
Then we go home
and await the ingenious means
our dead friends
devise to keep talking to us.

Sheila's medium is
her flare for marginalia
in those books
unpacked and shelved
among my own ten years ago.
Just this morning over coffee
she said, *Listen to this!*
her five-pointed star
penned in blue
beside *There are 84,000*
dharma doors
always available to wake us.

I reread that sentence
fingertip to star.
Her two penciled
question marks
above the chapter
On Reincarnation
waiting when I turn
the page.

The Daoist Lu Dongbin Crossing Lake Dongting
Painted Fan, Yuan Dynasty China

He was going to cross the water.
He was crossing on foot,
he was forever going to.

I was forever going to too.
Not the water, not the water,
I was going to cross the street
to ordinary happiness,

I was going to rest
beneath the twisted boughs
of the flowering plum
on a handscroll under glass
across the exhibit hall

but couldn't turn my back for long
on a monk who promised
to walk on water
in the thirteenth century.

I was crossing back to see him,
confined beside the left-hand edge
of a square silk fan, lines
of ink so spare—the painter's
held breath held yet between them.

I was going to light
the lantern in the next silk panel,
but not in this one.
I was going and always
planned to be the woman

eating pomegranates
beside the stream, fruit

of good fortune.

But he was going to cross the water
without even a small
wooden boat,

and I was going there—
with the wind filling his sleeves,
uplifting the long-held
hem of his robe,

his feet bare and poised
on the bank of great promise
for ever crossing the water.

II

Ask Anybody

I am carrying on. Ask anybody.
The only way to photograph wind
is to catch it cool-handed
stirring something—
night's white nightgown flying
pinned by a seam
to the clothesline.
On that secondhand
bicycle of childhood,
pumping hard
I could turn speed
into wind. I made it to save me.
Ask anybody. Wind
is God's great source
of subsequently
visible gestures.
I've been meaning to tell you,
the wind was so strong
on Tuesday I leaned into it
forging up the hill
to the orchard
as if pressing
through something,
as if moving forward
despite. Love was in the wind,
wind pushing in the other
direction. Even the trees
were carrying on.
And words, desiring each other,
aspiring to be gestures.
Forgive me, I'm always
trying to pin one down
on a page. Your left hand
cupping the right side

of my face
before the movie.
My chin at rest
in your palm.
You were drawing me
toward you. Ask anybody.

Uprisings

Eagle Lake, October

You just wanted to sit here
and watch what the breeze
knows how to do to the water.

Postcard autumn,
afloat and doubled.

You just wanted to sit here.

But what the wind picks up
when the wind picks up—

untroubled reflections
churned unrecognizable,

one mirror supplanting another.

You just wanted to sit here,
but the work of wind

is the history of uprisings—

furrows and crests
all mouthing at once,
a throng of untold stories

charging suddenly toward you.

Who are you to interpret
when the wind picks up
what the wind delivers to you?

You just wanted to sit
upright in a chair on the dock

believing nobody
occupies

the wind-rattled
empty chair beside you.

On the opposite shore
a mountain is stamped
unmoved against the sky—

sleeping torso on its back, head
buried beneath the treeline.

You sometimes live
at that same great distance
from everything.

But then the wind picks up,
breaching the distance.

The Brooch

It must have been someone else's, the gold-plated heart
I swallowed in the dream the night she swallowed the antifreeze
she'd always planned to swallow.

The nurse signed me in at night's local emergency room.

I borrowed her pen explaining on the page
how I put it in my mouth and drank
almost the whole glass of milk to ease it down easier.

She asked me why, but I had no answers.

When she got to the question of whether I'd fastened
the heart's sharp needle into its clasp, I shook my head.

Of course I was ashamed. Even I knew
you should always do this with costume jewelry pins
before swallowing them.

That's when she stopped looking at me
and pursed her lips. *Careless, careless. So much
trouble for someone so careless.*

I looked the other way for too long.
I hadn't phoned her back or woken soon enough.

The nurse disappeared but came back
with one straight-talking surgeon.

He could cut me open and *dig this thing out*
but it was so close now to my heart,

caught below the base of my throat
where the pain was, where sounds for words are born.

He said we'd just have to wait and see,
see what damage it does
as it makes its way through you.

I should have finished the whole glass of milk,
I was thinking. I should have.

Home

Innocent enough.

Following fresh prints
in a crust of snow.

A trail through the woods,
deep-rutted: mud thawed

then froze again.
Furrows of worry.

The fox, invisible guide.

Nothing to prepare you,
except your whole life,

for the bones of a past
that had no business being here.

Roof slit, slung lifeless.
Beams brought to their knees.

Floors cracked, boards snapped,
rot tumbling to the cellar hole.

This is the child's premonition:
the whole place leveled
by her father's next rampage.

Just enough left standing
to recognize—

a swatch of red geranium
still glued to the surviving wall.

Scavengers track through,
rescue what they can—

doors, casings, treads,
bricks chiseled
from the center chimney.

I want to pry the lintel with a crowbar
for a shelf, pile stones

to weigh down the dead
at the foot of the doorframe.

Retrieve the battered suitcase
pitched from a second-story
window into the brush.

On a stump of damp oak,
I sit shiva waiting for dark.

Leave this house
picked clean,
gutted by moonlight.

Half-Life

1.

Report said storm, but nothing
about being swept up fast,
caught open-mouthed, necks
craned at the sky. We only
say we expect bad news,
then a neighbor drowns
in his bath and all tubs
become suspect; the ordinary
only camouflage for peril.
Or the beautiful. The news says
planted inside a bouquet
a bomb blows the one
who accepts it apart.
Parting clumps of primrose
for weeds, I hear ticking
in the cinnamon fern. Mines
concealed now in borders
of nasturtium. Who says
we're entitled to refuge?

2.

What enters the imagination
remains there. My father
crosses the garden to pare
back brush. I want to feel
gratitude, as if his every gift
weren't a Trojan horse,
but all week the nightmares
rear up at his visit—
stubborn half-life of a child
who still wakes pleading

Somebody stop him.
Undisturbed by thunder,
he keeps shearing.
I call him in, my strongest
voice diluted in wind,
wind slapping the screen door
shut then sucking it open.

My Father Is Dying

All day inside the mind
they sleep the sleep

of hibernation. Four words
barely breathing.

I bundle up and take them out
under the brittle arms

of wintered trees
to say them a first time.

My is all it takes
to set the body

shivering. Emphatic,
my wants what it wants—

a still hopeful child's,
my, mine.

But within the spoken *father*
lies the unmistakable

farther, one letter
ever scarcely concealed there.

Is desires to linger when spoken
and end like the alphabet, *My father izz.*

A partial fact consented to
because *dying*

demands the tongue's
greatest effort, pushed up

into the palate and spit out,
a verdict delivered,

hard consonance of the *d*
as in *daughter*, which isn't said.

Each word coheres
into a momentary cloud,

a conversation
between frigid air

and the incomprehensible heat
drawn up from inside me.

My father is dying.
I say it three times

as if auditioning
for the part.

Evening Cove

The long dock can be reached
down a series of platforms and stairs.

Everything is trembling.

Even the hedges, roses gone late August
to their red hardened hips.

Everything is trembling
except the steady green flare
of the lighthouse in the distance.

* * * * *

I'm no quitter, he says, *but the docs say
I'm leaving this world.*

Our memories, my father is certain,
his one and only hereafter.

* * * * *

Small boats rock, harbored,
straining at the weight
of their anchors.

He'd fight with even a riptide
to the end.

Something's happening, he says,

composition for heartstrings.

Masts and riggings,
all rattle and clang.

* * * * *

Eighteen in his favorite photo,
head cocked and grinning
in starched Navy blues.

We had nothing, he'd brag,
meaning that nothing
that is something to have had.

Born to mop every deck.
Strong swimmer against
life's unremitting undertow.

His heavy hand made me
unsinkable.

* * * * *

He wakes full tilt from a day submerged
in sleep, diver surfacing
with his five newfound words.

I apologize, he says, *for disregarding you.*

Everything is trembling.

Brittle starfish pitched by storm-surf
found whole on the sand.

      * * * * *

A fistful of cold weathered stones,
his hand cupped in mine.

I'm afraid you'll forget me, he says.
I assure him that wouldn't be possible.

There's a world underwater.

His eyes pool with tears that fail to fall.

      * * * * *

In the dream he asks me to hold him.

Across the hospital room two nights later
he calls out my name.
Hold me, he says, *hold me*.

Landlocked a lifetime
inside the hard consonants

of *Dad,* I begin calling him
Papa. It's okay, Papa, it's okay.

Diver surfacing with her one
newfound word.

* * * *

The law is the law. Everything's trembling.

Where is it written, my father's sentence
to days or weeks of choking to death?

Something's happening, he says.
Can't you get me out of here?

The doctor winces when asked
for the something that is nothing
he would have.

* * * *

We pour out our hearts.
An ocean rises.

The same moon that drags out the tide
turns the sea heaving back to us.

But mercy sometimes corrupts
the unsuspecting.

The doctor returns, scribbles his name,
signing the orders.

* * * * *

The sea holds up the sky. Or is it—
the sky holds fast the sea?

There's an endless signature
scrawled between them we call the horizon.

That signature is trembling.

Prevailing winds sweep the cove, strands
pull free from the knot of my white hair.

A few drops of wine left in the glass
holding the moon.

III

A Long and Overdue Letter to Wendell Berry

> *I needed what was lost*
> *although I love as well*
> *the flow that took it.*
> —Wendell Berry, *Sabbath Poems* 2008 III

This morning in a late Adirondack September, I walked
the mile path to the lake through the woods, your Sabbath poems
in the pocket of my old denim jacket. When I say *old*,
you can rest assured, I'm pledged to words keeping faith
with their actual meanings.

I know it by heart, the trail's rises and bends, a rutted,
stone-studded passage of filtered light and layers of shadow.
And I know how it ends—spilling you suddenly out,
the wide eye of the lake startling no matter
you knew what was coming.

When I get there I usually sit cross-legged on the bank
until my rear can't take being any sorer. I read to the lake
whatever mood it's in: wind-riffed, rain-pocked, tranquil
glassy sky-mirror. But this morning a motorboat
was tied in the nearby boathouse slip.

It had been sitting unridden long enough
for the spiders to have accomplished weaving
their embodied sermons on interconnection; pail to wheel,
wheel to bow, bow to port, port to pail. Their daily work:
refuting the gospel of private and property.

So I pulled the boat and its vinyl-stuffed seat toward me,
climbed in and floated guiltless in its welcoming hull.
I read your poems to the then silent loons, the teeming lake
and the crow's unfettered accompaniment. I read to the crowns
of just turning trees; to the ever greens and all the lives
they go on sheltering here.

Meanwhile the winds had whipped up as I was reading
about the futility of building a better world
because how *could* the world *be* any better—
the boat knocking harder when I decided I'd better climb out.
I was lower than the slip the boat was tied to, so had to grip
and pull, maneuvering one leg up and across.

That's when your book fell between the boat and the slip
into the crack always opened between one world
and every other. Except for my moan,
there was only the sound of weight hitting weightlessness,
your pages soaked and swallowed, sinking utterly out of reach.

Probably it won't surprise you, but I wanted you to know,
your poems gave themselves up easily—less a drowning
than a homecoming, less an accident than the shared desire
of lake and language for each other. It was a perfect ceremony
of surrender. Even our own words never belonged to us.

Because Hope Has Only One P

Preposterous has two,
so I use it whenever possible

but only as it pertains
to improbable splendor
in its particulars.

This morning it was
one preposterously small boat
whooping up the placid lake

into stippled waves
thumping at the pilings.

A passion for P's
makes it easy to pick
your favorite anything.

Animal: porcupine.
Nut: pistachio.
French noun: parapluie.

How do you think
Prozac got so popular?

The poet is early primed
to parse past participles
and pinch back superlatives.

Prior to posthumous,
pish on this. Let irrepressible
play in P's

backyard plenitude.

That's where the pluck
comes from

to take on those P's we believe
we'd be better off without—

Plutonium, apartheid,
impoverish, corporate plunder.

Take heart, it's the P in despot
that patiently plots his toppling,
all those P's,

underground operatives,
pledged to the painstaking
piecework of our emancipation.

P's ply under the radar
protected by their reputation
for peace, polite, pretty please.

They pack pitchforks
for every possible impasse.

P's have telescopic outlooks.
They're at home with complexity,
placed right there

at the center of skeptical
to trip over.

Be a player, apprentice yourself
to the P chipping away

at complacency, persecute,
apocalypse.

Sketch that blueprint
for unprecedented parity, you
who are also indispensable

because hope has only
its one P

and there are no closing hours
in this world's shop
of perilous pastimes.

The President and the Poet Come to the Negotiating Table

I only agreed to compromise when it became clear
they were already stealing them again out from under us:
words, one at a time.

Okay, I said, like some ambassador for language,
facing him hunched over my yellow pad of conditions.

He was wearing his orange tie and with the graciousness
of ones who believe they have little to lose, he said,
There are far too many words anyway.

Okay, then, I said. You can have CONQUEST
and DOW JONES.

You can have BOMBS, but we want the SMART back.

This was fine with him. He had plenty of other words
for SMART, and would trade it for IMPERIAL and NUCLEAR.

TRADE is a word, I said, you might as well keep,
but don't touch SHADOW or PHENOMENA.

I gave up SOFT when paired with TARGETS
for the name of every bird. He said he'd consider
relinquishing CITIZEN for CUSTOMER.

I made my claim for CONSCIENCE, but he refused
until I sacrificed PERFECTION.

That's when he stood up shaking and wagging his finger at me.
He had spotted GOD upside down on my list.

Under no circumstances, he said, do you get GOD,
and only calmed down when he heard me announce

I completely agreed with him.

GOD, I said, must be returned to God.

But this wasn't what he had in mind.
In his mind were SHOCK and AWE.

SHOCK was the word to bring me to my feet,

because poets can rise up angry and shaking
for what they love too.

SHOCK, I said. You can have SHOCK.
But AWE—over my dead body.

Wind Breaks Into the House

through an open window—
drives papers off the desk

plastering paragraphs
against walls, stanzas

into corners of chaos
down the hall.

I unzip my sweatshirt
to let what the wind carries

of fields it passed over
sweep through me.

Tomorrow I will lift the pen

to a blank sheet of paper
from the wind-wracked hall.

Today, voice mail
will do my talking for me.

Leave a message.
Leave a message.

38th and Chicago

May 25, 2020

They brought him down
to the place where even wind
couldn't save him. It tried.

The wind gave him breath
for please, mama, please.

But between that knee
and his neck, there was
no open passage

for wind to wedge
between them.

Wind begged the mind
belonging to that knee
to come back

from the country
it was lost to.

But that mind
was drunk on dominion

and clenched tight
around

whatever had killed
the life-giving wind

inside him
a long time ago.

The Pandemic Blues

What doesn't add up.
What never did.

Chin up, served up,
screwed up,

we're picking up
all those pieces.

Buttoned up, bottled up,
corpses

piling up and tallied,
watching blown up

each night on screens
and channels.

We're up in arms
coughing up

the cover-ups
slithering

out from up
their sleeves.

We know by
wrapping it up

they mean
bringing it home.

Never Afters

Morning wind says *shush*
through boughs of white pine

but last night in a dream
earth's palette had no trace of blue.

      * * * * *

The cost of living
is indexed,

under the *B's* you'll find
birds of extinction.

Take, take, take,

soon what gives itself
dies to the giving.

You don't need commissioned
reports or headlines to know.

The new math is the calculus
of survival, birds by billions

blown with their songs
into the land of never afters.

      * * * * *

One breathless boy
wants answers—

So, where does
what disappears go?

You wanted him bowed
over notebooks
of empty, stacked
blue-lined horizons,

not choking on air,
backpack

crammed with inhalers
and the weight of the world.

* * * * *

We interrupt this program . . .

The oceans have soaked up
all the carbon dioxide they can.

That's Paradise burning.

That's us, still feuding,
en route

to hypothetical
futures.

Ashes, ashes …

blue marble
rolling to the edge

of time's long table.

Don't Call Me With Your News
for Jane Kaufman

Thursday after work
and the last days of a migraine,
after the physical therapist
traces my crooked vertebrae
to *issues of the heart*
and the rheumatology office
changes its mind
about taking new patients,
after the broadcast
numbering veterans
home with no legs,
killing themselves
or their wives,
and the mechanic
calls to report
I need two new tires
and a rotation,
after the high school play
about school shootings,
and the kid in the West Bank
who agreed to blow himself
up at the checkpoint
stares up at me
from under a headline,
I open a carton in today's mail
from a sculptor I sent
one measly poem to,
her quirky clay angel
encircling one full-figured dove,
and think, to hell
with bootstraps,
for surely we need
to swoop in most days
and save each other.

Points of Departure

Between the bungalow
and the sea,
the long hedge
of winter is packed
with sparrows
facing an ocean
churned to acres
of unrest—

the promise
of old platforms
for deliverance
revealed
by gale winds
as only the barely
audible chirping
of bystanders.

Thud of water
against obstinance
of stone, of surf
chipping away
at the foundations.

I drove to the coast
to write an elegy
for the war dead
and the newly
fallen sycamore.

I dream about
the dream of fruit
sleeping inside
gnarled trees

even now
in the nearby
hardened orchard,

like justice
in the dead of winter
waiting to ripen.

Stories That Tell Us

This is one of those stories about a woman who turns herself
begrudgingly around. The main character, at first,
is the front of a late February blizzard.

She is inside it driving at the end of a too long day. To be fair,
it's important to say it's after dark and she is hungry.

The radio isn't playing in this story because
steering through a whiteout requires listening,
and she wants to get home without an accident, squinting,
chest pressed up into the wheel.

She wants to get home though no one's waiting
except for her worthy opponents: a small tribe of mice
she rails against while envying their shameless brand of genius.

She's tired, that's why, she tells herself,
she doesn't exactly register that crazy soul hitchhiking
on the icy road's night shoulder.

But this is a story about a woman who crawls to a stop,
pulled in idling across the mouth
of someone's disappearing driveway.

She's hearing that voice in the cold that sounds like her own
but addresses her as *You*. *You know he must be freezing.*
You know anyone out on this ice could skid and kill him in a flash.

This is one of those stories where a woman cuts a deal—
she'll make the U-turn and drive back,
make another U-turn and drive by him.

If it's that good-natured nearly blind man from town,
who's forever trying to cajole her into having
coffee when they meet at the post office, she'll pick him up.

She's already begun excusing her wish to overlook him,
reminding herself she's weary and how the last time
she gave him a ride he'd left smears where his pants
were not quite covering his not completely wiped behind.

But even tired, hungry and chastened by the smell
of her own stinginess, this is a story about a woman
who still thinks she is going to do someone else a favor
by doing someone else a favor.

Beneath a mask of crystal slivers, sure enough it's his face
framed by a parka's orange hood.

When that door opens in her story the blizzard enters with him.
And while he apologizes and thanks her and thanks her
again, she recognizes that self-congratulatory flicker
in her small heart. *I am a good person, I am a good person.*

In second gear inching them forward, he's just settling in
when she loses control for a moment downhill.
Only then does it come to her that two frightened souls
on the slippery road makes for companionship.

This is the story of a nearly blind man who hitchhikes
daily at the mercy of friends and strangers,
who hums half a mile before asking if she's ever
written a poem about a storm.

In that silence where she's still trying to remember,
he says he has one, clears his throat and starts reciting it.

That's when she sees this is going to be a story
about grace coming to the least deserving—this man almost
singing the ballad about a boat endangered in a *wild, wild sea.*

When she asks who wrote it, thinking
Longfellow or Tennyson, he tells her, smiling, *me.*

This is one of those stories that happens, if you're lucky,
to you. One of those stories that tells you who you are,
then goes on telling you.

IV

And Still, Dawn

The full moon lingers
over my right shoulder
while winter's sun rises.

Pastel horizon
under a procession
of sheer lingerie,

frayed wisps sailing
ever so slowly by.

Nothing rushed.
A tutorial in the art
of gradually.

Thanks to the perch
of this hill, I'm parallel
with the airborne.

Geese. Blue Heron.
Crows.

Without spectacles
all the things of this world
are soft as milk glass

and further out of reach.

Barer trees.
Fewer places to hide.

Provocation for tenderness.
Waves of it . . .

My aging body,
the welcoming shore.

Carlotta at Home
Abiquiu, New Mexico

1.

With only instinct for compass
and wounds demanding
a vast horizon, she sought out
this mesa encircled by mountains
like any woman overtaken
by a call from midlife
to start over. She didn't build
so much as raise this house
up from sand into air,
dowsed ledge for water
and then, defying
whatever odds were left
to defy, planted seven
plum trees for seven friends
death came too early for.

2.

In the desert, light reclaims itself
as noun: a presence
not for serving the illumination
of other things but for being itself,
a sovereign character in the greater story.
The plum tree saplings are young,
still sure light exists only for their ripening.
And who'd argue with the bravado
of spindly branches in the desert
bearing the preposterous
weight of all their plums?

3.

When Carlotta holds out a basket
pretending to wonder
if I'd care to harvest the plums,
we both know the real question:
Can I bear the weight
of such happiness in a chore?
First plum in the basket,
next plucked for my mouth—
tithing warm juice and flesh,
a few dropped for birds.
Quicksilver sky. Hardy pit
at the heart. The fruits
of a woundedness transfigured,
Carlotta humming behind me.

4.

Everything in the desert
testifies to the improbable.
Late afternoon winds fly in
carrying the blackbirds
Carlotta says roost every night
in the crowns of the seven plum trees.
Behind the wind, a dark bank
in the distance is driving
rain across the desert toward us.
The plum leaves quiver
offering up their earthly applause.

Duet

The crow comes to the bare branch
and stays put

just outside
the ten-paned window.

Sleet comes too, mid-April,
winter clutching time—

a tangle of stiff limbs
impersonating the lifeless.

The crow grasps what is brittle,
scored bark inside a sheath of ice.

The first lines of a stanza,
frozen on the wooden desk between us.

Nothing wants to be said.

The crow is indifferent
to all things melodious.

We can just go on
seeing each other

because the branches continue
to hold back their green wings.

It's subtle. The crow tilts
its head. I tilt mine.

We see what we see
through the perch

of the other's seeing—
a woman

affixed to her own branch
who appears to be living

inside the confinement
of only one pane.

Eyes set to eye,
I rise in slow motion

and cross the room
as if to demonstrate

I am also a creature
made for freedom.

The crow steps into air
and hoists both wings

as only an afterthought,
threading a path I can't see

through a turmoil
of twigs and branches.

My one wild wing,
mind of its own,

begins shamelessly
waving

to the crow
who mattered

more, leaving the poem
unfettered to find itself.

Stanzas of Rome

1.

The cypresses are too large
for the courtyard
but not for the sky, the sky

that has room for desire
with its consequences.

In a language I cannot yet
understand, everyone here
is trying to explain this to me.

2.

From across the piazza, I can see
into the church's open doors,

but from out here it's all darkness
except for the flecks
of candles burning.

I'm going to leave
the cafe's smallest table
and follow

whatever in there
is calling to me.

The church bells
ring every quarter hour.

It's too late
to underestimate

what they're trying
to explain to me.

3.

Everyone borrows the flame
of a stranger's prayers
to light their own—

I find a place for my lit taper
where there's room left
in the votives' iron grid.

Misjudging the invisible—
the heat in empty space
surrounding fire—

I singe the cuff
of my blue sweater.

Hours later, forgetting
the source,

sniff around
for something burning.

4.

The museum's guide
on Renaissance painting

describes in English
the application
of *deaf colors*.

The consequences of desire
lead to accidents,

to missing *muted*
as the obvious
mistranslation.

But it's too late—

I've adopted a pantheon
of deaf prophets,
saints and angels.

5.

I am trying my friend's patience.

It's Palm Sunday
and we've ordered Campari
beside the Church
of Santa Maria Trastevere.

It's served in glass funnels
filled with the juice
of blood oranges.

She wants me to explain
how I can go on praying
without knowing who
or what I'm praying to.

I love her more then
than I know how to love
God yet, for asking.

I say, it wouldn't help to hurry.
I want a God whose name
I can pronounce.

I say, the cypresses
are too large for the courtyard.
But not for the sky.

6.

In silent pews
others are praying

under flaming frescoes
out of mute desire.

I'm stationed
on the portico steps

writing out words
to make them legible
to the deaf sky.

The mute prophets
and the deaf angels
can smell something burning.

A mob of songbirds
living in the cypresses
are trying to explain it to them.

Coming Unspooled

Who lives here?
I'm asking

the now opened
sewing box

where threads
of ageless color

stare up, entangled,
loosened from their spools.

That's how it is, I mean
in my mind,

disentangling thoughts,
names, knots,

where sometimes
only scissors

and wasted thread
are the answer.

Even without
shaky hands

disassembling disorder
is tricky business,

not to mention
threading a needle.

If not for nostalgia
and my weakness

for mending the threadbare,
I might throw out

the basket of years
and start over.

Daily Dialogues With the Pieces

meditations on a painting by Carolyn King

1.

It had to come apart. The bluebirds
on a limb, the limbs pulled
from the sky, the sky disassembled
into shards of blue and splinters of light,
the sun's setting fire still setting
dispersed into fractions of itself
clinging to pieces of horizon.

2.

She'd already created disorder
but she needed more turbulence,
more light wedged between things
too large for the small territories
mapped out to contain them.

The painter lays her hands
over the surface of the painting,
listening for fault lines.
Fault. Faulty. False.
Without faltering, she saws
the world into the puzzle it is.

3.

The Dictionary of Word Origins
says the origin of puzzle is a puzzle,
perhaps derived from the obsolete verb
meaning interrogate or perplex
but possibly from another
meaning picking out the best bits.

4.

Every bit necessary. Not a fraction
of divine source in each
distributed

according to virtue
or good fortune.

5.

Humpty Dumpty sat on a wall.

What did all the king's horses
and all the king's men
do with the pieces?

Did anyone think to consult
with the Queen?

6.

They said the straight edges
would help us frame order
out of the anarchy
of loose jagged parts: the early
jigsaw puzzle of childhood.
Duly prepared, we marched in
trusting the box we were each given
contained all the pieces.

7.

Early morning,
cedar waxwing's
cold collage—

feathers scattered
by predator, by wind,

origin of one name
experienced firsthand—
yellow band of wax

hand painted
across the tip
of every tail feather.

Collecting them,
collecting them,

as if to breathe
life back
only required

finding all
the pieces.

8.

You might have thought
this was the other story,

the one about rubble, violence,

the day-to-day darkness
undoing the world.

But not today. Today
the pieces are dictating
the headlines:

Coming Apart, Prerequisite
For the Work of Astonishment

Conversations break open,
rivers of space

take up residence
between them—

spacious sky surrounding stars
and the yet-to-be-named
constellations.

Forget wedging one
into the edges of some
perfectly designed other.

Your hands, my hands,
reconfiguring the pieces.

The Sea's One and Only Word

From the beginning, the sea
has been collaborating

with the bluff, the sandy shore,
the clattering stones, calling to us,

Belovèd . . .

Can't you hear it? The conspiracy
of tides, shifting forces of the moon,

moody winds over the surface?

The whitecaps have been delivering
the sea's one and only word through time.

Standing before the brimming commotion,
we might mistake the message

falling at our feet
for inconsequential sound.

Our ears have heard things, after all,
that were bound to discourage hearing.

But the sea is never discouraged,
because it has its one and only word

and because it speaks to us
on behalf of all creation.

Listen. Can you hear it?
Inside the incoming tide.

Acknowledgments

My thanks to the editors of the following journals and anthologies where many of these poems first appeared, sometimes in slightly different versions:

The American Journal of Poetry:
"My Father Is Dying," "Because Hope Has Only One P"

Painted Bride Quarterly: "Half-Life"

The William and Mary Review: "Aurora's Actually"

Cathexis Northwest: "Ask Anybody," "Blue Yonder," "Sheila's Marginalia"

Broad River Review: "A Long and Overdue Letter to Wendell Berry"

Red Rock Review: "Carlotta At Home"

Except for Love: New England Poets Inspired by Donald Hall:
"Duet," "Picking Raspberries," "First Acts"

Abstract Magazine: Contemporary Expressions: "Uprisings," "Indebted to Wind," "Home," "The Daoist Lu Dongbin Crossing Lake Dongting," "Points of Departure"

Pinyon Review: "And Still, Dawn"

The Other Side of Sorrow; Shock and Awe War on Words; Peacework:
"The Poet and the President Come to the Negotiating Table"

Saint Katherine Review: "The Sea's One and Only Word"

Persimmon Tree: "Momentarily Untitled"

Joy of Aging Anthology: "Coming Unspooled"

Syracuse Cultural Workers Women Artists Calendar:
"Don't Call Me With Your News"

The Poetic Dialogue Project: "Daily Dialogue With the Pieces"
appeared in response to and coupled with Carolyn King's painting
installation "Putting the Pieces Back Together"

*   *   *

I am grateful for fellowships from The National Endowment for
the Arts and The New Hampshire State Council on the Arts, and
for residencies at The American Academy in Rome, The Mac-
Dowell Colony, Hedgebrook, Wellspring House, The Hermitage,
and most especially The Blue Mountain Center, where many of
these poems were hatched and revised.

My tender thanks to Ella Moye-Gibbons for her contribution to
"Picking Raspberries," to Aurora Ellis-Hopkins for instigating
"Aurora's Actually," and to Jane Kaufman for inspiring "Don't
Send Me Your News."

I am indebted beyond measure to Karen Latuchie who generously
read these poems over many years, and believed in them. I could
not have asked for a more incisive and thoughtful reader. Her
love, imagination and friendship sustain me.

My deep gratitude to all who read this book as a manuscript and
offered their time, insights and encouragement, especially
Kathleen Aguero, Deborah Brown, Martha Collins, Jessica
Ellis-Hopkins, Alice Nye and Stephen Tapscott.

My heartfelt thanks, as well, to those who offered the companion-
ship and spaces of refuge necessary to bring this book into being,
among them Harriet Barlow, Cile Beatty, Betty Burkes, Barry
DeJasu, Evelyn Ellis-Haines, Helen Fitzgerald, Patricia Gianotti,
Catherine Hoffman, Sandra Ileuscu, Eric Lister, Cassandra
Medley, Laura Slattery, Sue Morin, Rachel Vaughan, and the late
Vincent Harding and Peter Ediger.

Finally, my gratitude to Chris Jerome for her full-hearted gift of
editing, to Danielle Nelson for her perfect cover image, and
especially to my publisher Jeffrey Haste at Deerbrook Editions
who takes poets under his generous wing.